Charles William McCabe

Poems of Home and Fireside

Charles William McCabe

Poems of Home and Fireside

ISBN/EAN: 9783337254438

Printed in Europe, USA, Canada, Australia, Japan

Cover: Foto ©Thomas Meinert / pixelio.de

More available books at **www.hansebooks.com**

POEMS

OF

HOME AND FIRESIDE

———

BY

CHARLES WILLIAM MCCABE.

Dedicated to my Father and Mother

. . . . .

Who, during a life of toil, retained the elements of true living and made home happy and a blessing to their children, by their kindness, cheerfulness and Christian bearing in the face of many discouragements and hardships.

THE AUTHOR.

PROEM.

Oh, is there on earth, a picture more fair
    Than the family gathered round the fireside.
Not the family alone but the nation is there,—
    The brain and the brawn we so pride.

It is by the fireside great lives are made,—
    The influence brought to bear there.
Oh, home, thy dear memories never shall fade,
    But with time and great nations shall wear.

The Toilers.

HOW pleasant on returning home from toil,
　　To know that those best loved thy com-
　　　　ing wait.
What peace and happiness after a day of moil,
　　To meet thy wife and children at the gate.

Affection's kiss goes round, and on each face
　　The light of love and sweet contentment rest,
While the fond father for a little space,
　　Clasps his sturdy offspring to his breast.

No towering walls of marble palace holds
　　Ties dearer than the toiler's humble cot.
No truer life its blossoms there unfolds,
　　Than that which blooms the poor man's
　　　　family plot.

Taught in the days of youth to serve the Lord,
    And live in quiet unpretentious ways,
No wicked strife is there to bring discord,
    But peace and happiness lengthen out their
        days.

What honest cheer the toiler's coming home,
    To head the table and bless the hard-earned
        bread,
And pray for those without such comforts roam
    The world at large, unhappy and unfed.

How sweet to hear the children's merry voices,
    As through the house they caper with delight.
Oh, how the parents' honest hearts rejoice
    As with modest pride they gaze upon the
        sight.

At nine the clock has struck the hour for rest,
    The children sleep within the trundle-bed.
Oh, kiss them tenderly and own thyself much
        blest,
    For joy that comes to those who truly wed.

Blest are they ere life is on the wane,
  Who understand the secrets of true life,
If from all vice and folly do refrain,
  And solace find in husband or in wife.

Seek where you may no lasting joy you'll find,
  But in the narrow circle here laid down.
No ties of wealth or fame are strong enough to
    bind
    Together hearts,where dissention's shadows
    frown.

The law of love is ruler of the home,
  And honest toil the greatest nations make.
Think not you 'll find, no matter where you
    roam,
  A different law divined for thy own sake.

Contented be with the toiler's humble lot,
  Free from pomp and ostentatious life,
Let thy home be the workman's tidy cot,
  Thy best friends thy children and thy wife.

The Rain.

OH, I love to hear the rain
    On the roof and window-pane,
As it patters, patters down,
    Clothing earth in a wet gown.

Lost in dreams or gentle slumber
    Flit the hours without number,
When the patter of the rain
    Beats on roof and window-pane.

How the shadows light and darken,
    When to rain and wind I harken ;
What ghostly figures then appear,
    What strange voices do I hear.

Now I start from gentle slumber,
  Turn to the clock and note the number
Of the hours that stole away
  While King of Nodland held his sway.

Out of Nodland to day dreaming,
  Slippered feet and grate-fire gleaming,
Thus I love to hear the rain
  On the roof and window-pane.

Now through palace halls I stray,
  Culling life's roses all the way.
Proud ambition drinks her fill,
  But something more is wanting still.

Now in fancy proud ambition
  Bows her head in deep contrition,
And the common walks of life
  Seem more worthy of man's strife.

For all great things loose their prestige,
  And the ages leave no vestage
Of the things that have been,
  Of the temples made by men.

So in strange lands do I wander,
   Life's grave problems love to ponder,
When the patter of the rain
   Sounds on roof and window-pane.

The Two Rivers.

DEDICATED TO AGE.

THE river of life grows less wide,
   There is no ebb or flow of tide,
Dark clouds have fled from out the sky,
Life's cares and troubles pass me by
A gleam of light I see beyond,
That in my soul find glad responc
Rent in twain is the vapored screen,
Immortality's river is rolling between.
Lo! in the distance as in a dream,
I see the boatman crossing the stream.

The Passing of Night.

THE gray and restful twilight
  Hangs softly over the earth,
Evening steals on and the firelight
Plays merrily around the hearth.

Night is here and the darkness
  Hides the world and its sin,
Brings a haven of rest to the weary,
  Wings to the burdens of men.

Midnight comes and the city
  Lies silent, breathing deep,
While white-winged guardian angels
  Their silent watches keep.

Morn is near and the darkness
  Flies from the light of day,
And the white-winged guardian angels
  Flit silently away.

The Cares of Life.

WHEN the cares of life o'erpress me,
    When day is changed to night,
When joy is turned into sorrow,
And the world seems aught but right,
Then in my phantom barque I enter,
And with the tide drift on the sea,
Drift far on the unknown river,
Drift into eternity.

Unspoken Prayer

AT night or day,
　　At work or play,
　Rejoicing or in despair,
Deep in the heart
Unbidden start
　Unspoken prayer.

In the quiet of night,
Thoughts of wrong and right
　Increase or lighten our care,
Which ere it be,
From our hearts flow free
　Unspoken prayer.

[17]

It is the lot of men
That all must sin,
  All have sorrow to bear,
And passing them by,
We hear them sigh
  Unspoken prayer.

When comes that day
And we're called away,
  Called to dwell over there,
We 'll find in God's heart
  Ready to start
A record of unspoken prayer.

———

Faces.

———

EACH life 's a history, but human faces,
  Upon which time has left deep traces,
Are mirrors of the heart's distresses,
Which to the world divers tales confesses.

Tom's Letter to Bill,

OR THE BROTHER CANDIDATE.

———

DEAR BILL: I 've just now took in hand
   my pen,
To write a few lines to you agin,
And as this letter 's from me to you
Please excuse the writin' and spelin' two.

As a boy there was none like you, dear Bill,
Who could harness a team and go to mill,
Who dun the chores in the early morn,
In a day husked a hundred bushels of corn.

'T was I who used to lie in bed,
While you, dear Bill, went right ahead
A'tendin' the cattle and doin' the work
Which I, dear Bill, so loved to shirk.

[19]

When in the field we used to hoe,
If the weeds were strong you dun my row.
'T was always so, 't was just your way,
And I can't help thinkin' of it to-day.

How easy my life you used to make,
My burdens upon your shoulders take,
How in a hundred different ways
You helped me in our boyhood days.

But this ain't the reason I 've writ to you,
For this of course I often do ;
But they say at the Grove,—the people say,
That I, dear Bill, am in your way.

I mean, of course—about election day,
That 's what the people at the Grove all say.
Say, if they were brothers they 'd hate
To be agin each other as a candidate.

Well, your family bigger 'n mine, dear Bill,
You 've four more mouths than me to fill,
And I reckon you 'd the sheriff be,
If, as the people say, it were n't for me.

So now, dear Bill, to tell the truth,
And to square the debt of my early youth,
I ain't agoin' to run agin
A man who is my nearest kin.

Tomorrow, dear Bill, is election day,
And I 've writ a letter to the paper to say :
" That I, Tom Jinkins, brother of Bill's,
That lives at the Grove, County of Mills,

" Have concluded not to run agin
A man who is my nearest kin,
And asking the people of the County of
    Mills,
Not to vote for Tom Jinkins, the brother of
    Bill's."

Saying : " I 've just concluded, before it 's
    two late
Not to be a sheriff candidate ;
But that my oldest brother, the one named Bill,
Is in the race for sheriff still."

[21]

Tell the boys at the corner — make them un-
    derstand—
That I 'm two busy a tillin' my land.
I 've a crib to build, and must dig a well,
And that will take a right smart spell.

I ain't a man of affairs, no how,
All the boys who know me must this allow.
But some other time, mebbe, I won't hate
To be a sheriff candidate.

Twilight Notes.

THE air is so soft and fragrant around me,
 The evening comes stealing o'er valley
  and hill,
But the silence is broken, so softly, so gently,
 By the sound of sweet music and my soul
  seems to fill.

'T is the notes of a guitar so sweetly is sound-
  ing,
 Afar o'er the valley on the still evening air,
In tremulous tones its voice is resounding,
 By the soft summer breeze wafted hither
  and there.

As I list to the strains so sweet and spell-
  binding,
 My thoughts speed away on lightest of wings,
And a calm that's the saints' seems my soul
  enter-winding,
 My heart and all nature in harmony sings.

[23]

The Old Willow Tree.

OH! the old willow tree that stands in the
    meadow,
Its low drooping branches throwing a deep
    cooling shadow,
How oft have I sought thee in the heat of the
    day,
To rest and to dream the noon hour away.

In thy shade oft in childhood, (Oh! bright,
    golden hours,)
Have I pillowed my head on a wreath of wild
    flowers,
And with the song of the lark and the hum of
    the bee,
What sweet rest it was 'neath the old willow
    tree.

'Neath thy low bending branches, tree of
  beauty and splendor,
I first met my love, so fair and so slender.
'T was long, long ago, sweet Amy and me,
First plighted our love 'neath the old willow
  tree.

The flight of the years has whitened our hair,
And life's cares and sorrows oft seem hard to
  bear.
Yet not a year passes, but my Amy and me
Renew our first love 'neath the old willow tree.

Oh, old willow tree, we still fondly cleave thee,
For old memories sake we 'll be sorry to leave
  thee,
But we hope when we 're gone, my Amy and
  me,
They 'll lay us to rest 'neath the old willow
  tree.

Nutting Song.

OH! there's joy in the Autumn when the
frost's on the ground,
And the nuts from the trees are falling
around,
To rise with the sun and off to the woods,
Where the frost-bitten nuts are shedding their
hoods.

Oh! what joy in the Autumn when the trees
are aglow,
With red-tinted leaves kissed by Autumn's
young snow,
To go to the woods ere the frost's off the
ground,
And gather the nuts that lie scattered
around.

Oh! it 's jolly in Autumn with the boys and
   the girls,
To go to the woods where the bushy-tailed
   squirrels
Are carrying nuts to their holes in the
   trees,
To keep them from starving during winter's
   cold freeze.

What unstinted pleasure after a day of real toil,
To return home at night heavy ladened with
   spoil,
To crack nuts and tell stories 'round the
   kitchen's warm fire,
Till the clock on the mantel strikes the hour
   to retire.

Oh! there was nothing in Autumn that gave
   me such joy,
As going a nutting when I was a boy,
To rise with the sun and off to the woods,
Where the frost-bitten nuts were shedding
   their hoods.

An Autumn Dirge.

DESOLATION 'S reigning,
  Autumn leaves are staining
The earth so brown and sere,
Earth so bleak and drear.

November winds are blowing,
Like rain are dead leaves sowing,
The earth so brown and sere,
Earth so bleak and drear.

Everywhere wild winds are wailing,
Death and snow are trailing, trailing,
O'er the earth so brown and sere,
Earth so bleak and drear.

The Church Bells.

———

LIST to the church bells ringing,
  Far up in the steeple high,
List to the church bells ringing,
Their music floating by.

Far out o'er hill and river,
Retreating and advancing,
Charming ears that listen
Their melody entrancing.

Oh! sweet, sweet ringing bells,
All nature stops to listen,
Thy deep-toned mystic swells,
Sweet ringing, ringing bells.

When I'm Dead.

DEAR, on the day they dress me,
  My shroud so stiff and white,
Will you, my darling, kiss me,
As I lie so cold and quiet ?

And dear, on the day I am buried,
Will you quietly let fall a tear ?
In your heart will you carry my image,
As sadly you turn from my bier ?

Will you sometimes bring a sweet violet,
And lay on the grass-covered mound,
As a token of love you bore her,
That 's crumbling to dust in the ground.

And when I enter God's Kingdom,
Shall I leave the portal ajar ?
Shall I set a light in heaven's window,
Whose brightness shall outshine the star ?

A light on the sill of God's window,
That shall burn as a symbol of love,
A symbol of glory that 's Heaven's,
A symbol of God who is Love.

That thou from thy lowly-laid dwelling,
May see the light from afar,
May know that your darling is waiting,
Waiting by the portal ajar.

And when the light in God's window burns
    brightest,
When your barque 's moored to eternity's
    shore,
Will you seek among the angels' dear faces,
For the face of your darling once more ?

Drifting Apart.

TO W. E. M.

DEAR friend, I fear we are drifting—
                          far apart,
That distance and old time are sifting—
                          each heart,
Tho' in my visions thy face and thy image—
                          oft appear,
Oh! forgive me if thy friendship seems—
                          less dear.
Is it because unwittingly a tie—
                          was broken ?
Or was it a kind word left—
                          unspoken ?
Take my hand, dear old friend, it is—
                          reaching ;
If I 'm the offender thy forgiveness I 'm—
                          beseeching.
Let no false note, time or distance—
                          keep us apart,
Remember days gone forever—
                          friend of my heart.

The Poet.

THO' his feet trod the earth,
  His head rests on a star ;
Tho' 'mong mortals had his birth,
  His spirit wanders far,
Wanders, wanders restlessly,
  The corners of the earth,
Seeking spheres blissfully
  Where his soul had its birth.

Tho' 'mong men has his being,
  Dwells in fancy's land ;
Through the universe travels
  With the Gods, hand in hand,
Mediator of earth and heaven,
  Heir to estate Divine,
To men, the earth, angels, Heaven,
  Oh ! poet, both are thine.

[33]

To Mary.

I SEE the blue of your eyes, Mary,
  I see the blue of your eyes,
Tho' distant far, as the glimmering star,
  I see the blue of your eyes.

I hear the sound of your voice, Mary,
  I hear the sound of your voice,
Tho' the ocean wide do us divide,
  I hear the sound of your voice.

I see the smile on your lips, Mary,
  I see the smile on your lips,
Tho' mountains high sever you and I,
  I see the smile on your lips.

[34]

I see the blush on your cheeks, Mary,
  I see the blush on your cheeks,
As red as the rose it comes and goes,
  I see the blush on your cheeks.

I see the blue of your eyes, Mary,
  I hear the sound of your voice,
I see the smile on your lips, Mary,
  And my heart would fain rejoice.

But I know not if your love be mine, Mary,
  I know not if your love be mine,
Tho' the ocean's tide bear you to my side,
  I know not if your love be mine.

The Wreck.

———

THE ocean's wild waters are rolling, rolling,
   A ship's muffled bell is tolling, tolling,
The death knell to hearts, unconsoled, uncon-
   soling.

Tumultuous waves o'er the good ship are flying,
A hundred brave men are dying, dying,
In the ocean's dark waters their still forms
   are lying.

Like a draught from the breath of the universe
   breathing,
The wind o'er the ocean's wild waters is
   cleaving,
Like sighs from the earth the waves are up-
   heaving.

O'er the face of fair Heaven the storm-clouds
 are creeping,
On the ocean's broad breast the wild waves
 are leaping,
Far beneath the wild waves the ship's crew
 are sleeping.

Through a rift in the clouds the bright stars
 are peeping,
The untroubled moon in a calm sky is sleeping,
In a hundred sad homes widows and orphans
 are weeping.

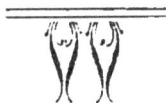

The Wanderer's Return to the Scenes of His Youth.

AFTER years of wandering the world
around,
Weary at last I sit me down
On the outskirts of my native town,
And with haunted memory gaze around.

On every side some familiar sight,
Gives to my heart new joy or blight.
At every turn there greets my view,
The scenes my truant boyhood knew.

I see the cot where I was born,
In rustic beauty all forlorn.
Dear spot where flowers their spring-buds
swell,
I knew and loved thee once so well.

The old school house is standing still,
I see its roof beyond the hill,
The belfry rising above the trees,
That 'bout the ground sway in the breeze.

Boys and girls still romp around,
Together on the playing ground.
I hear their laughter's echoing resound,
As it lingers faintly o'er the roofs of the town.

Those joyous hearts, how little they know
Of the ills of life, its toil and woe.
To them how bright life's horizon gleams,
How sweet, how sweet are youthful dreams.

Ah! there 's the bell, how sweet its ring,
How oft it 's called me from the spring,
Where at recess I used to drink
The bubbling water from its brink.

To the woods near by how oft I 've stole,
There in deep shades to dream and loll.
How oft my brother Ned and I
Flat on the ground there used to lie.

To list the murmuring of the stream,
The singing lark or jay's shrill scream.
To hear the hawk's exulting cry,
While mounting swiftly towards the sky.

But ah! for me those days are past.
Aye, life itself is fading fast.
But still 't is "bitter—sweet" to dwell
Among these scenes I once loved well.

But those I loved, loved most dear,
Father, mother and one more dear,
Who gave to me her heart and hand,
All dwell together in the silent land.

Here in the glen between the hills,
Where nest the lonely whip-poor-wills,
Where ferns and dewy grasses wave
Each lie forever in the grave.

And through the evening's gathering gloom,
I read their names upon the tomb,
Fast from my eyes flow bitter tears,
Effusions of long pent-up years.

Standing sadly under the darkened sky,
The years of my life again roll by,
Scenes of the past linger in my brain,
Memories' faces live again.

☀

A Life's Retrospection.

———

THE night was fair,
Fragrant the air,
With roses sweet.

The bright moonbeam,
Like silver streams,
Lit the street.

A dimpled child,
Lisped and smiled,
As it slept.

A maiden fair,
With golden hair,
Dreamed of love.

[42]

A happy wife,
Sang psalms of life,
In her joy.

A mother wild,
Wept o'er her child,
Lying dead.

The night was fair,
Fragrant the air,
With roses sweet.

Meditation on Death of a Friend.

AND so he's dead,—dead!
Can this be he who I knew so well;
this cold, senseless clay, he, who but yesterday was as I am now,—a living creature, with
power of thinking, seeing, doing, and now,
alas! is dead, oblivious to the world, gone.
Where?
Who knows. His image is still before me,
but cold, motionless, unconscious, and with
marble lips and closed eyes, separated forever
—for eternity, from that we call life. And
what is life? Is it not as mysterious, as fath-
omless as death? Lives there one, or ever
lived who knows from whence it comes, why
here, whither bound? Yesterday this inert
clay possessed life. Today, it has departed.
Yesterday those heavy lids were lifted, and his

blue eyes beamed upon the world and me. He spoke kind words, smiled, ate, drank, and—lived. Today he is changed, dead, gone. And where? Theology cannot tell me. Science leads me far hence, and learning in all its various channels, but teaches me the futility of attempting to bridge this mysterious gulf. I have studied the theology of many sects, have measured the distance from the earth to the sun; know the orbit of every planet drawn earthward by invention, can foretell the exact moment of the eclipse, have chained the thunderbolt and utilized it to the good of mankind; can trace the currents of the ocean, and tell the exact moment of its ebb and flow; have vaulted mountain tops, or with the wings of an eagle; have wrested a million secrets from nature, yet I, even I am helpless, and like him, like all the world must die, must go, but where?

To the Antelope.

THOU swift-footed beauty,
  Timid child of the plain,
Did man do his duty,
Thou never wert slain.

Oh! thou bonny-eyed darling,
To wild nature wed,
Thy eyes like the starling,
A bright luster shed.

Thy home 's on the prairie,
The desert 's thy bed,
But soon from the prairie,
Thy herds shall have fled.

The horn of the hunter,
As he rides o'er the plain,
Is a dirge to thy mates,
Whose herds he has slain.

Oh! thou swift-footed beauty,
Timid child of the plain,
Did man do his duty,
Thou never wert slain.

My Needs.

A CABIN to live in, a few acres of ground,
Happy me with these possessions found,
A plow, a horse, some good seed corn,
And I 'm the happiest mortal ever was born.

The great and rich live in ease and grow fat,
But I do not envy them for that.
My few acres and seed-corn may not yield
   wealth,
But plain food to eat, and better—good health.

Add to this some good books, a retreat in the
   forest.
I want nothing else, tho' my fortune 's the
   poorest.
With plain food, robust health, and good books
   to read,
Neither body nor mind will soon go to seed.

As a still greater blessing give me a good wife,
And I 've all the luxuries man needs in life.
This Kingdom I crave kind nature 's the donor,
And it 's better than wealth, ambition or honor.

America.

AMERICA! America! Thou art our native land.

We are thy sons and soldiers, and by thy flag we 'll stand.

For thee we 'll march to battle, for thee we 'll gladly die,

For thee we 'll leave our home and friends, thy enemy to defy.

For thy honor as a Nation, for the glory of thy name,

We 'll maintain the laws and liberty that sounded first thy fame,

And whether in war or peace, which ever it may be,

Thy sons will ever rally in the cause of liberty.

In the cause of independence (for which our grandsires fought and won),

Liberty's message has descended from father unto son.

And for the nation our fathers founded, for the land that they made free,

Their sons will ever rally in the cause of liberty.